More Amazing Dinosaurs

and Other Prehistoric Animals

Written and illustrated by **John Cartwright**

Watermill Press

Stegosaurus

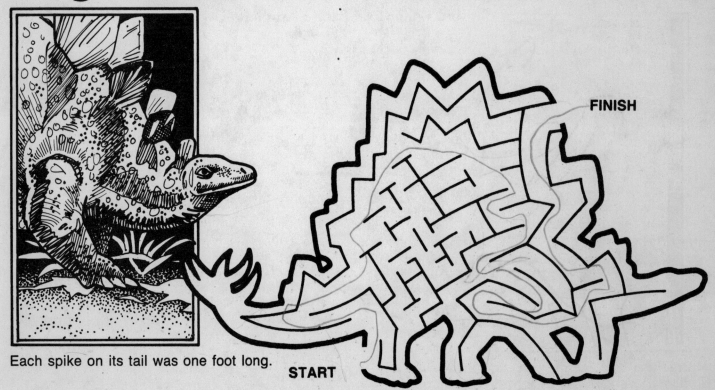

Each spike on its tail was one foot long.

START

FINISH

Brachiosaurus

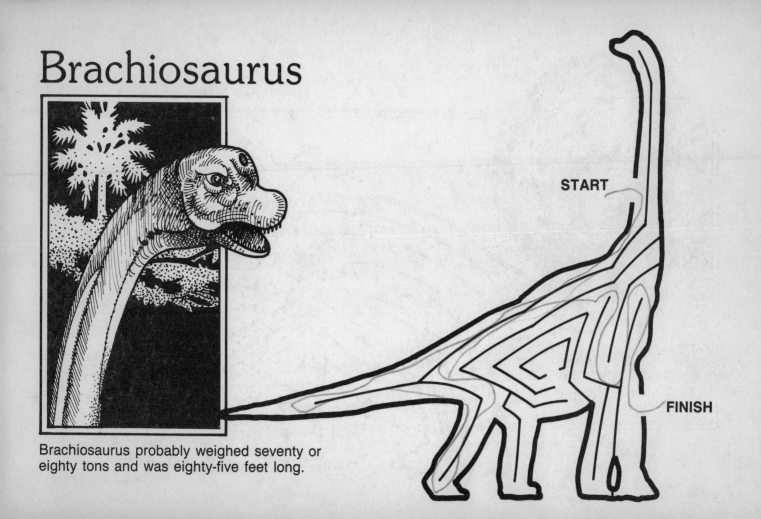

Brachiosaurus probably weighed seventy or
eighty tons and was eighty-five feet long.

START

FINISH

Cynognathus

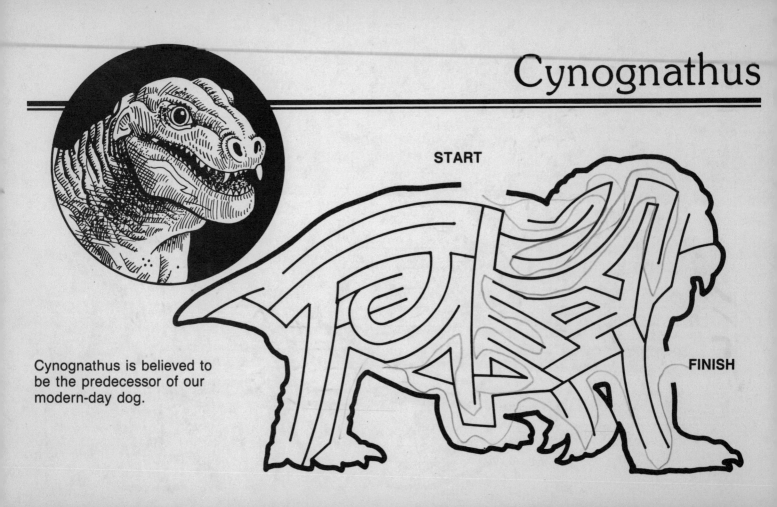

START

FINISH

Cynognathus is believed to be the predecessor of our modern-day dog.

Archelon

Archelon was a North American turtle
twelve feet long.

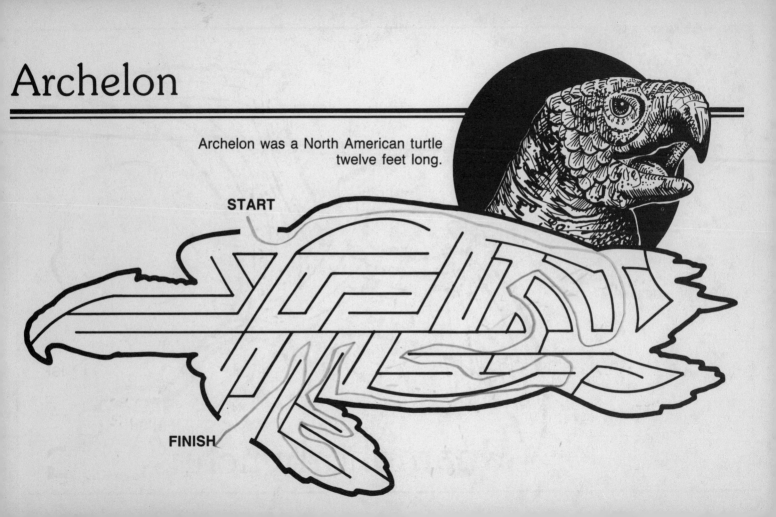

START

FINISH

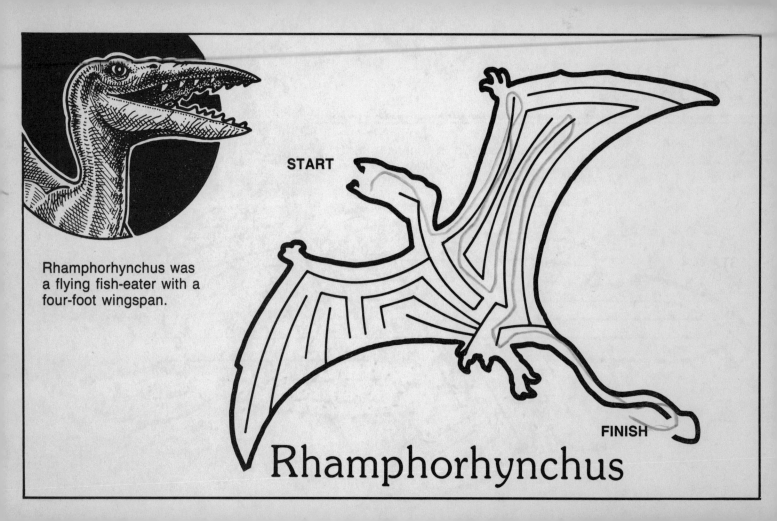

Rhamphorhynchus was
a flying fish-eater with a
four-foot wingspan.

START

FINISH

Rhamphorhynchus

Styracosaurus

Styracosaurus had long spikes on its frill edge, plus a two-foot horn on its nose.

START

FINISH

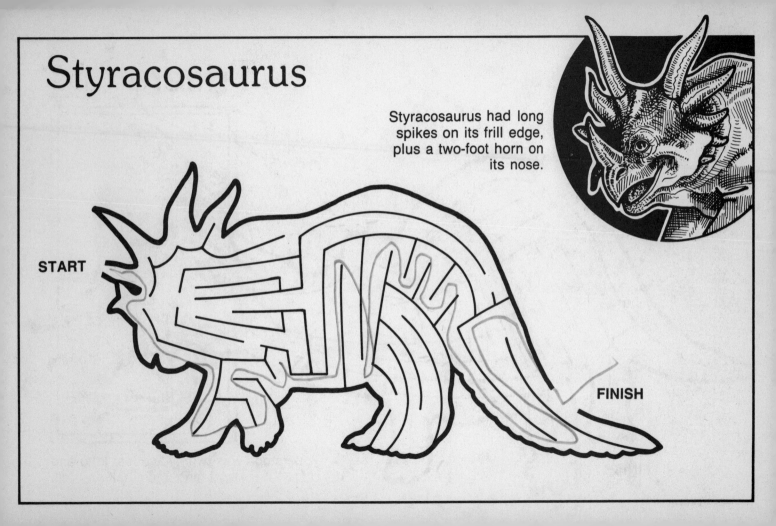

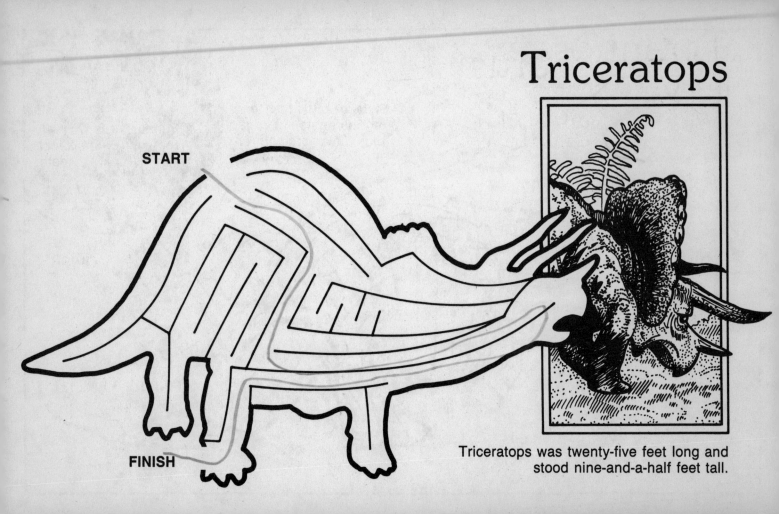

Triceratops

START

FINISH

Triceratops was twenty-five feet long and stood nine-and-a-half feet tall.

Styracosaurus

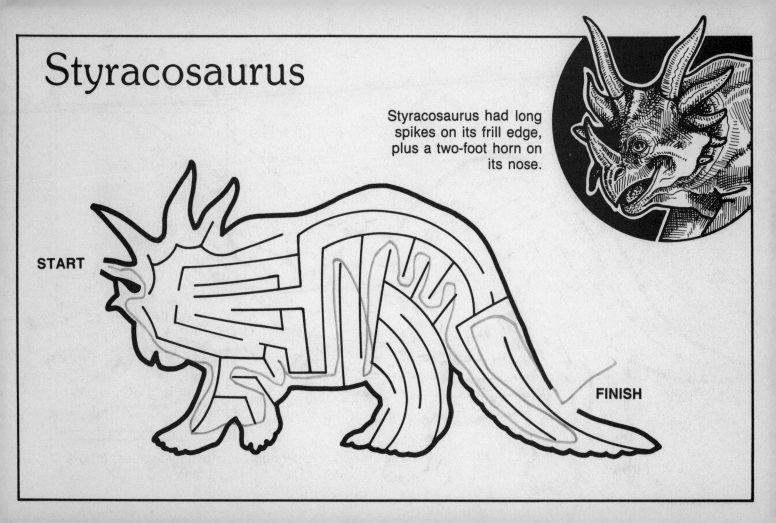

Styracosaurus had long spikes on its frill edge, plus a two-foot horn on its nose.

START

FINISH

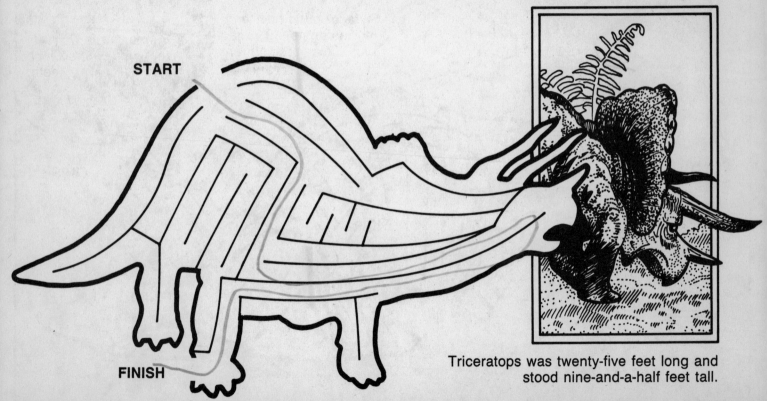

Triceratops

Triceratops was twenty-five feet long and stood nine-and-a-half feet tall.

Tyrannosaurus

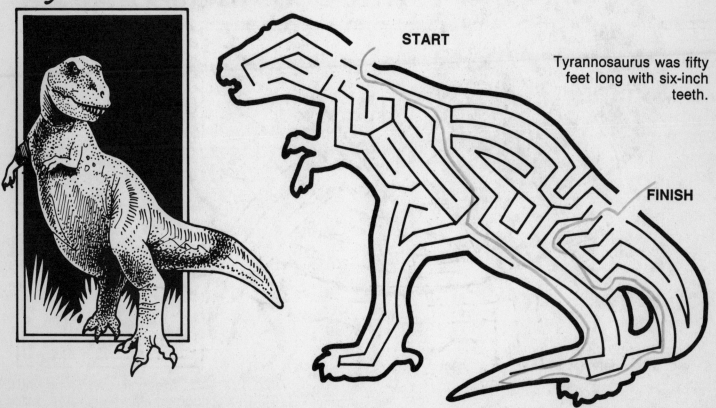

START

FINISH

Tyrannosaurus was fifty
feet long with six-inch
teeth.

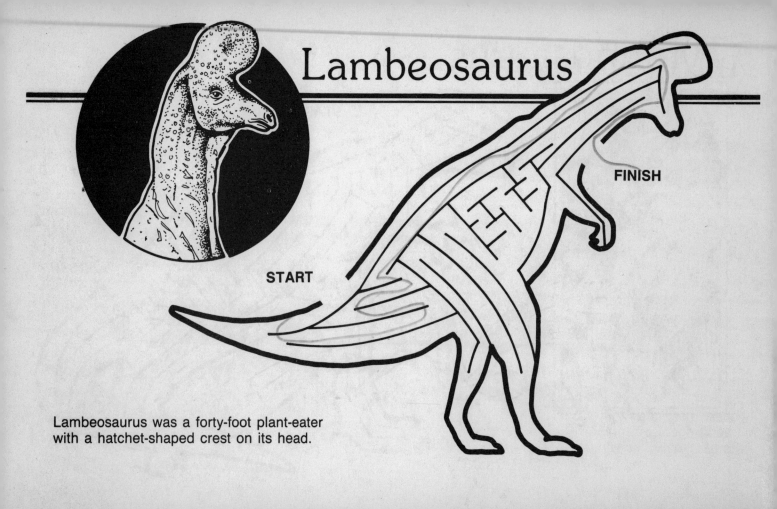

Lambeosaurus

START

FINISH

Lambeosaurus was a forty-foot plant-eater
with a hatchet-shaped crest on its head.

Archaeopteryx

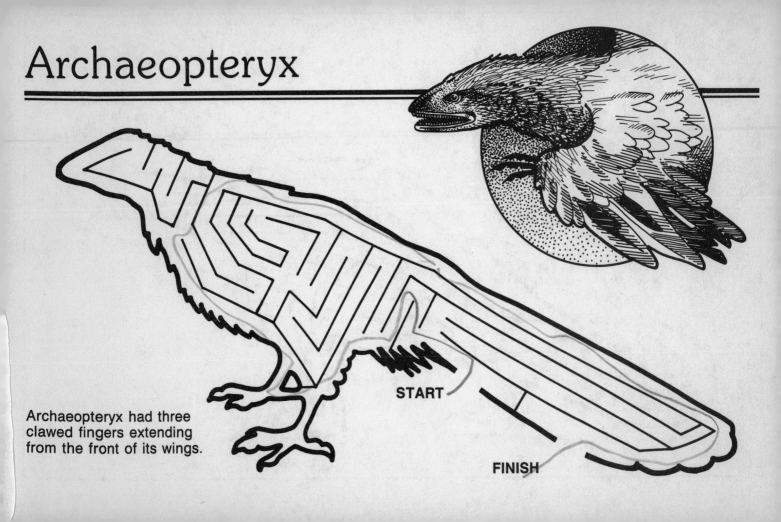

Archaeopteryx had three clawed fingers extending from the front of its wings.

START

FINISH

Allosaurus

Allosaurus could unlatch its jaws like a snake in order to swallow large chunks of meat whole.

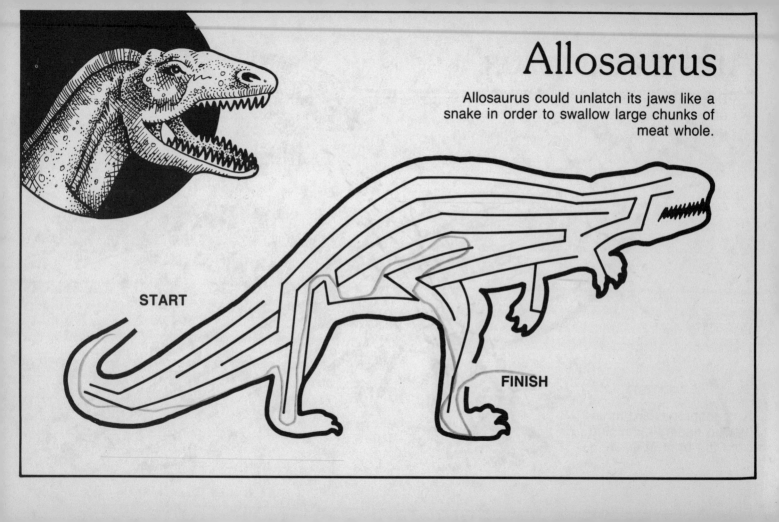

START

FINISH

Archaeopteryx

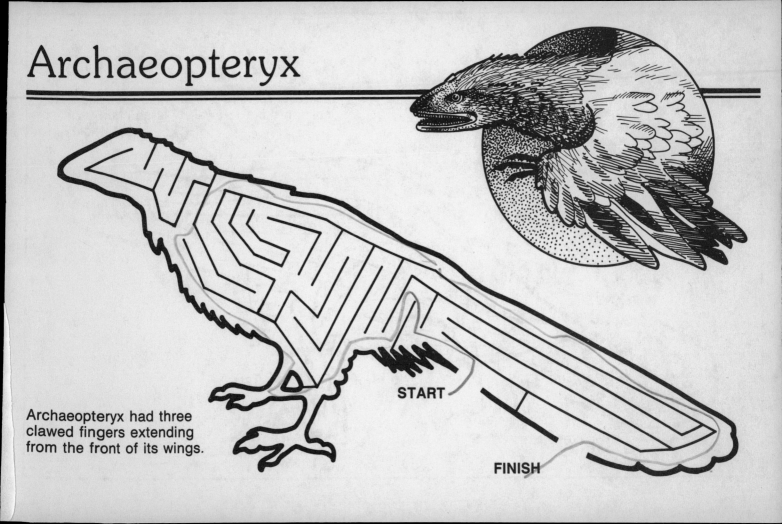

Archaeopteryx had three
clawed fingers extending
from the front of its wings.

START

FINISH

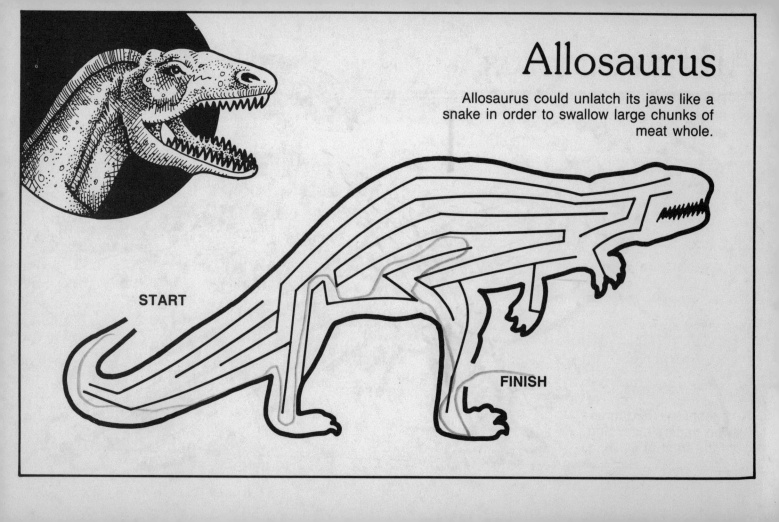

Allosaurus

Allosaurus could unlatch its jaws like a snake in order to swallow large chunks of meat whole.

START

FINISH

Deinonychus

Deinonychus most likely hunted in packs and thus was able to bring down animals larger than itself.

START

FINISH

Plesiosaurus

START

FINISH

Plesiosaurus, a marine reptile measuring ten feet long, fed on small fish and other sea animals.

Ankylosaurus

START

FINISH

Ankylosaurus, covered with bony plates
and leathery skin, also had a bony club of
a tail to defend itself.

Dilophosaurus

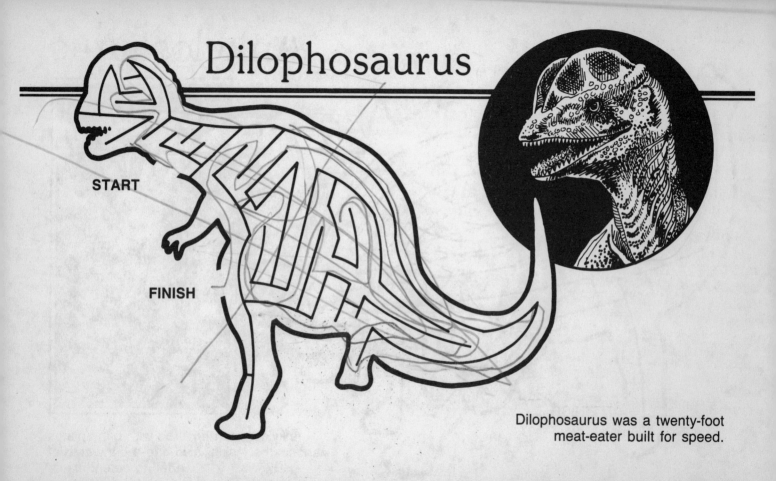

START

FINISH

Dilophosaurus was a twenty-foot meat-eater built for speed.

Chasmosaurus

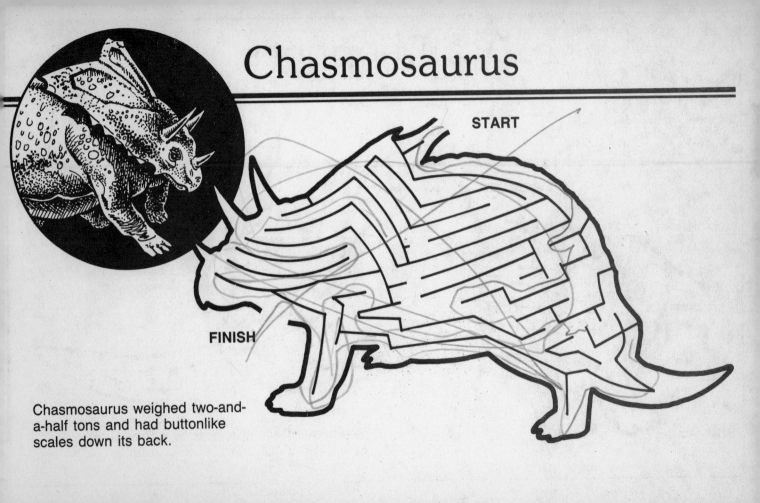

START

FINISH

Chasmosaurus weighed two-and-a-half tons and had buttonlike scales down its back.

Acanthopholis

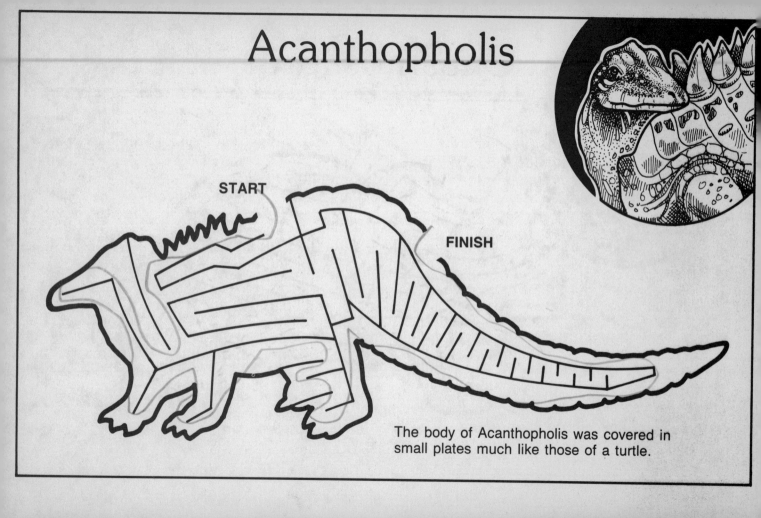

START

FINISH

The body of Acanthopholis was covered in small plates much like those of a turtle.

Elasmosaurus

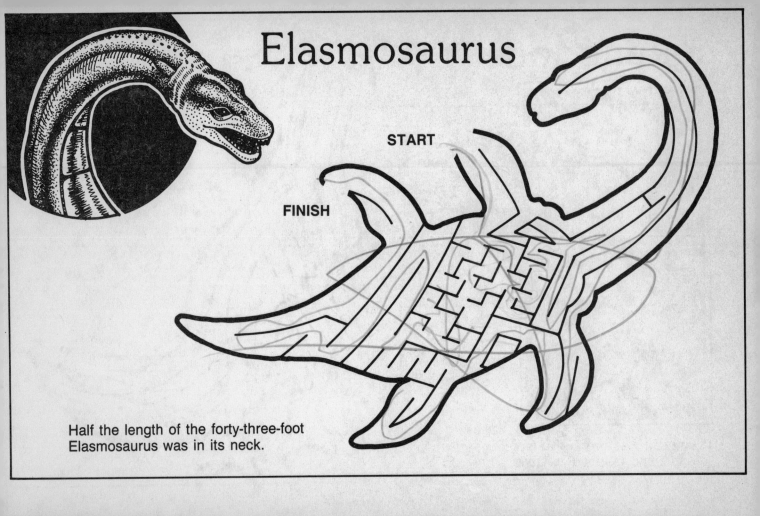

START

FINISH

Half the length of the forty-three-foot
Elasmosaurus was in its neck.

Iguanodon

Iguanodon was twenty-five feet long, fifteen feet tall, and weighed five tons.

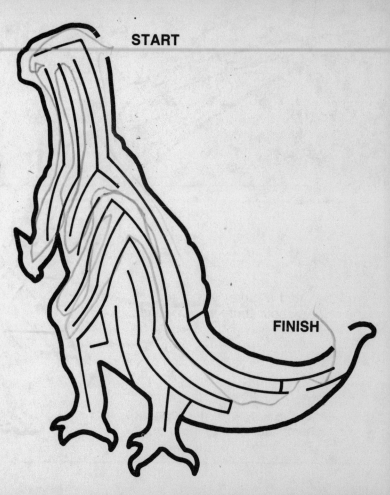

START

FINISH

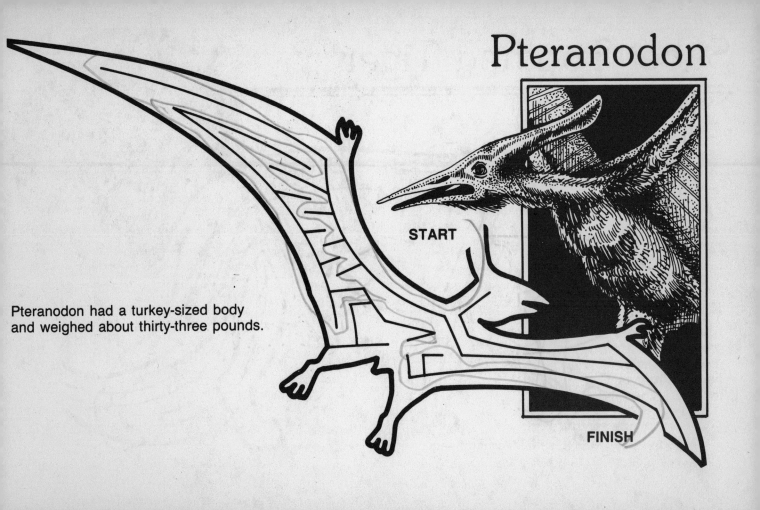

Pteranodon

Pteranodon had a turkey-sized body
and weighed about thirty-three pounds.

START

FINISH

Saber-Toothed Tiger

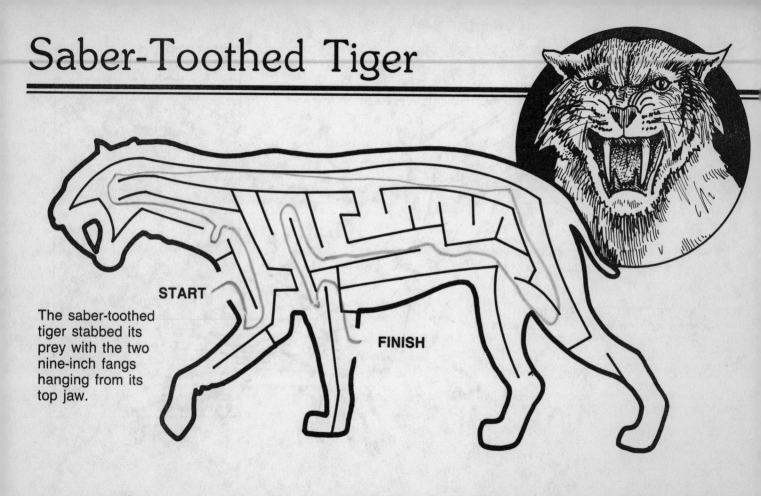

START

FINISH

The saber-toothed tiger stabbed its prey with the two nine-inch fangs hanging from its top jaw.

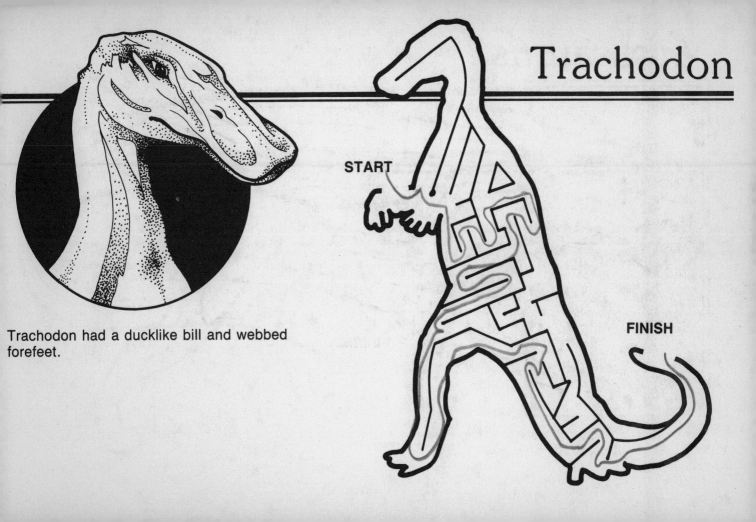

Trachodon

START

FINISH

Trachodon had a ducklike bill and webbed forefeet.

Mosasaurus

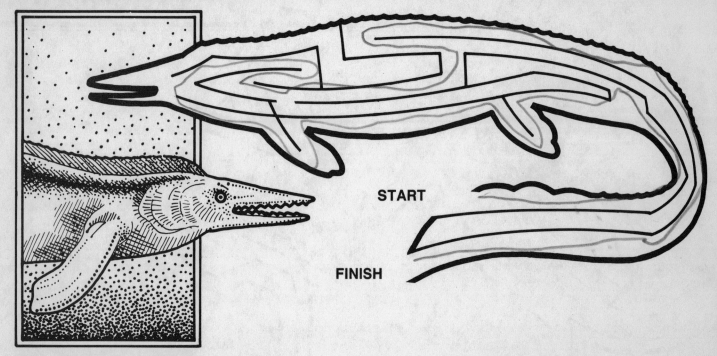

START

FINISH

The jaws of Mosasaurus were four feet
long and full of sharp teeth.

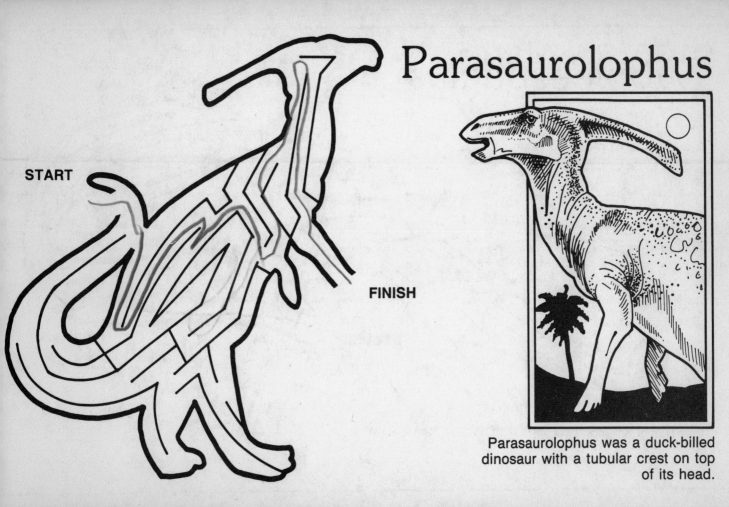

Parasaurolophus

START

FINISH

Parasaurolophus was a duck-billed
dinosaur with a tubular crest on top
of its head.

Euoplocephalus

The tail of Euoplocephalus ended in
a bony club with two spikes on it.

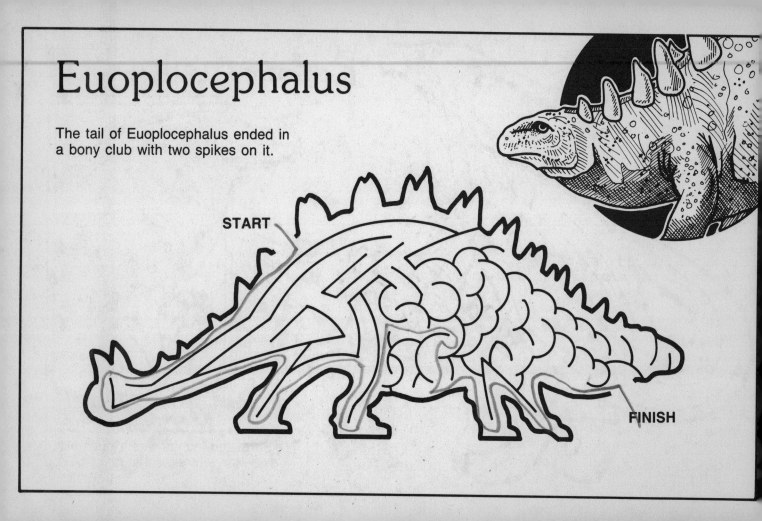

START

FINISH

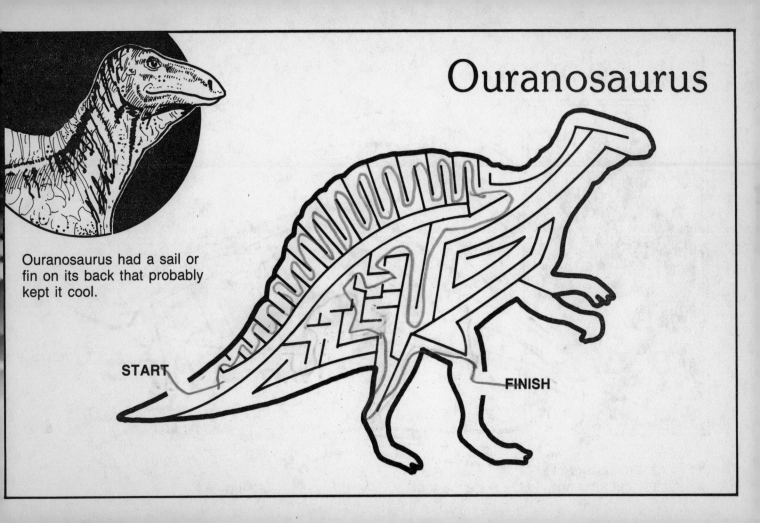

Ouranosaurus

Ouranosaurus had a sail or fin on its back that probably kept it cool.

START

FINISH

Diplodocus

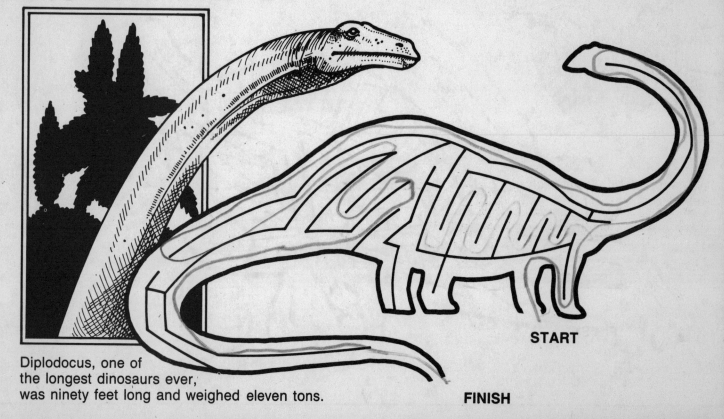

Diplodocus, one of
the longest dinosaurs ever,
was ninety feet long and weighed eleven tons.

START

FINISH

Dimetrodon

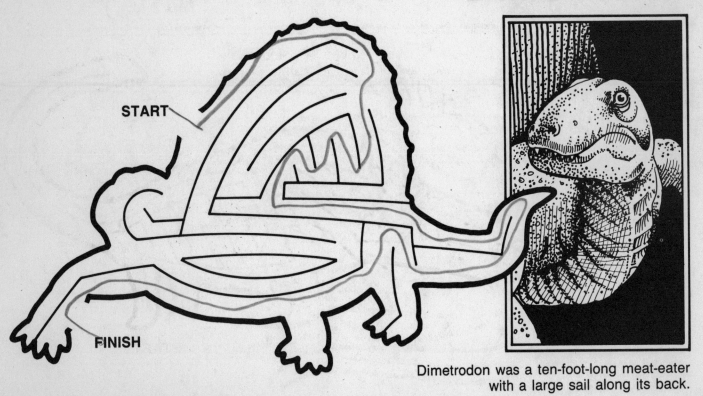

START

FINISH

Dimetrodon was a ten-foot-long meat-eater with a large sail along its back.

Ichthyosaurus

Ichthyosaurus was a thirty-foot flesh-eater that gave birth to live young.

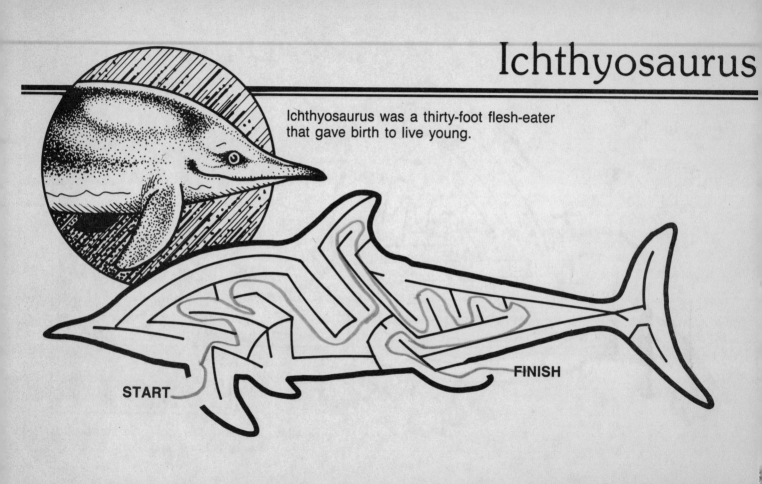

START

FINISH